THE AGE OF DISCOVERY

THE AGE OF DISCOVERY

Navigating the World's Great Explorations

B. VINCENT

QuantumQuill Press

CONTENTS

First Printing, 2024

CHAPTER 1

Introduction

Welcome to the initial stop on a journey through the Age of Discovery. This will be an exciting adventure through a time in history that reshaped the modern world. Four hundred years ago, the great European powers sought to expand their empires through trade with the rich Orient. To accomplish this, it was necessary to find a way to the Orient that was not only expeditious but safe; thus, the Age of Exploration began. In this age, explorers had to endure the vast Atlantic and Pacific oceans and find a way across the many continents. Some exploration was done with the intent of discovering new lands for the mother country like Christopher Columbus, and some was done with the intent of finding a path to a land with riches, like Hernando Cortez. Underlying the many different goals that these explorers sought to achieve, there was a consistent theme of the subjugation of native peoples and the acquisition of their riches for the betterment of the conquering nation. This theme is echoed loud and clear through the explorations of China/East Asia and the well-documented conquests in the Americas. Through compelling primary sources and insightful secondary analysis, we will see how the events in this age have shaped the modern world and discover why the Age of Exploration is a period of history that no one should soon forget. Step aboard, and let the journey begin!

CHAPTER 2

The Motives for Exploration

The longing to get a route to the Far East is an aspiration that overwhelmed the early and advanced civilizations in times. The medieval Europeans looked for the unfathomable wealth and culture of the Eastern World as an alternative to avoiding the Goths and also the Muslims. In this, the Eastern World is referred to as being fairly a conceivable social change. The civilization of China and furthermore India, as well as the Spice Islands, fulfilled the European idea of a generalized Golden Age. Facts and additional reading on these places were sloppy and there was no solidified European thought of a glorious age compared to when Rome was in its prime. The possibility of gaining outlived the death and looking as another social order was what consolidated Europe's insight of making a push to attain Asia with the undertakings and failure of finding a North West or North East Passage with an investigation of European death.

While the essential motivation of the first colonizers of the New World is portrayed by idealism and creativity, the pioneers of the European Age of Exploration demonstrated a significantly more mind-boggling scope of inspirations. The fundamental goals of imperialism and colonization were supported by open mission for wealth and prizes that involved the rulers as well as the genuine oceanic undertakings who accompanied them. The innovative developments occurred in the fields of cartography and navigation were led by a longing to achieve the rooted times of legend. The mission for learning and the pursuit to comprehend the obscure are referred to by both avaricious scholars and basic mariners. These inspirations may nearly be analyzed and outlined as following.

CHAPTER 3

Early Explorations

Although it is unknown whether the rumors of the metals were true, Egypt had strong relations with the Minoans. This could have been the influence for Minoans to later travel to Egypt and build the Palace of Knossos. This journey to Crete marks the beginning and end of the Minoan civilization's exploration, and the Palace is an indicator of a successful voyage.

One of the earliest recorded explorations was done by the Minoans of ancient Greece. The story tells that the King of Egypt hired a group of Minoans to bring back valuable metals, which were rumored to be in a region known as "The Land of Caphtor". The Minoans went on to discover what is believed to be the island of Crete and the language of Linear A, which has yet to be translated. This language is also said to have been adapted by the Mycenaeans of the Greek mainland, thus being the first writing system for ancient Greece.

In this section of the essay, we explore the in-depth details and expeditions of explorers before the "Age of Discovery". It is, in fact, discovered that most of the exploration done by early civilizations was not for the sake of exploration, but rather for food and resources. With that being said, there were a few significant journeys taken by these ancient cultures that helped to set the stage for later exploration.

3.1. European Explorers

The discovery made by an Italian in the service of Spain would soon affect all of Europe. John Cabot, a Genoan mariner who resided in England from 1495 until he disappeared in the North Atlantic in 1498, attempted to reach the Asian sphere from a more northerly route than Columbus. Although his voyages were unsuccessful in a geographical sense, they still shaped history. In 1494, the King of Portugal asked the Pope to ratify the Treaty of Tordesillas. This treaty divided the heathen world into two spheres of influence for Portugal and Spain. The world would be divided along a meridian 370 leagues west of the Cape Verde Islands, with anything discovered to the west or east of territories held by Portugal belonging to Spain. Any other lands were up for grabs. This explains the lack of impact of the French Columbian adventures. In 1524, with the consent of King Francis I to plunder papal land, the Florentine Giovanni da Verrazano obtained permission from France, where he expected to find employment. He landed in Kingston, NY at the end of the year.

The voyages of Portuguese explorers, who were essentially driven by their desire to find alternative routes to India and escape from the Muslim Turk captivate, profoundly changed history. In 1488, Bartholomeu Dias rounded the Cape of Good Hope on the tip of Africa, and 10 years later Vasco da Gama reached India. With this feat, they expanded the world, and the impact of their arrival was still felt as late as 1750. The Spanish quickly followed the Portuguese example and sought a route to Asia by sailing west. Christopher Columbus attempted to reach India by sailing west in 1492, but instead, he landed in the New World. In the following year, Pedro Alvares Cabral reached the Brazilian coast. Seeking to solidify its claim, Spain relied on these settlements to bypass other European powers. This new land could possibly provide an elusive solution to the never-ending struggle with Islam.

3.2. Asian Explorers

For centuries, European scholars pondered various concepts of world geography. The ideas of Ptolemy, the ancient geographer, were based on a theory that the earth was divided into temperate and torrid zones. The only lands known were those of the temperate zone in the northern half of the earth, to the east of the Atlantic Ocean. The implication that there could be unknown land in the southern half of the earth was very intriguing. In addition, he spoke of a great southern continent. These ideas fired the imagination of Portuguese explorers. It was their hope to find a direct route to the spices of the East that would bypass the Muslim lands and Venetian middlemen. An alternative to this was to find the fabled great Christian kingdom of Prester John who was thought to preside over a wealthy and friendly nation who could assist with the expulsion of the Muslims from the Holy Land. He too was thought to reside in the East. Both of these quests held a promise of finding new allies for a great crusade. And there was also the speculation of finding the aforementioned unknown lands in the southern half of the earth. The first person to take up these indirect routes to Asia was Bartolomeu Dias. In 1487, he sailed to the southern tip of Africa, which he rounded, proving the possibility of a sea route to the east. This had solved the problem of the Muslim blockade of the overland routes. 10 years later Vasco de Gama, who had been influenced by the ideas of King John and was in want of a more direct route to Asia, stopped at the Cape Verde islands themselves, hoping to find one of the islands, as described by the great story of the seven voyages of Sinbad, which would blow him to some unknown part of the world. Realizing his near heresy, he prayed and on the fourth day, caught the winds that blew him on a straight course to the southern tip of Africa. Upon the return, Di Gama was, by request of King John, to build a fortress at the site of what was called Elmina, to offer protection to the voyages to India. This was to be the now permanent tactic of establishing a trading post to ensure the safety of the voyage. He later landed in Melinde, despite having treated the ruler badly in a previous visit. He died there.

CHAPTER 4

The Impact of New Technology

An intriguing grand theory has been proposed that psychological trauma induced among Indians through their sudden and catastrophic encounter with Europeans may have led to the fatal introduction of "alcoholism as a Flight into Oblivion". This thesis cannot be conclusively supported or refuted, but it does suggest some of the deeper and more powerful effects of European technological superiority.

The most important military development of the age was the widespread use of firearms and the evolution of the tactics that maximized their effectiveness. Guns firing iron balls first became a practical weapon for seaborne expeditions; the Portuguese employed them against Moors, Africans, and Asian coastal peoples, while the more technologically conservative Chinese only briefly used cannon in the 1520s to repel an invasion by the Japanese. In the long run, the military uses of firearms gave the Europeans a huge advantage over the Indians and other peoples of the Americas and Africa who were to be encountered in the future. Traditional weapons such as swords, and especially armor proper to various warrior elites, were often nearly useless against massed infantry armed with pikes and accompanied by gunners. Yet, it was not the guns but rather native firearms and the disorganization of their peoples that caused the collapse of many American and African elites in the face of European military offensives.

A Portuguese invention, the caravel, was a ship that was both lateen-rigged and square-rigged. This allowed the ship great maneuverability, especially useful in beating to windward (sailing into the wind). The Iberians also developed the astrolabe, as had the Greeks and Arabs, but the device was especially useful to sixteenth-century navigators, who used it to plot the courses they had previously only estimated. These navigational advances were so important to later generations in Europe and other continents that it was long believed that the explorers had succeeded through a "revolution" in scientific knowledge, possibly by secret instruction from ancient sages, or interaction with extraterrestrial beings. In reality, the knowledge was gradually and selectively drawn from several non-European civilizations, and the practical effects of the changes have often been exaggerated. Still, the new technologies gave the Portuguese a crucial advantage over other nations in the search for a direct route to the sources of the highly valued spices of Asia.

Navigation provides a clear example of these general patterns. The Chinese had discovered and used the compass to aid maritime navigation during the eleventh century, and the technology was diffused to the West through the Arabs. Yet, during the fifteenth century, European mariners developed compasses with glass bottoms that allowed the magnets to align more precisely, and thus more reliably indicate the direction of the Earth's magnetic pole.

The impact of new technology: The Portuguese and Spanish explorers of the fifteenth and sixteenth centuries ushered in a new age of world history. The technological impetus for this transformation was mainly European, as was the willingness to take great risks in the pursuit of potential gains. The most fundamental changes after 1450 were the use and further development of older technologies, a greater commitment to overseas exploration, and a willingness to draw on the ideas and resources of other civilizations.

CHAPTER 5

Exploration of the Americas

The Old World inadvertently introduced communicable diseases to the New World. While American food products became popular in Europe, foreign diseases took a heavy toll on American Indian populations.

In addition to population increase, exploration led to changes in the diet of both hemispheres. The Old World gained many new types of food from the Americas. Maize, manioc, and the potato became very popular and were, at the time, a far more efficient form of food production than any, and far easier than the methods Europeans had been using. However, the exchange was imbalanced. While the Old World gained a variety of new foods for the first time in its history, the New World only gained livestock.

Population growth in Europe before the exploration of the Americas was stagnant; from 1450 to 1660 it only grew by about 25%, however population growth after 1500 in the Americas was substantial. As King Philip II of Spain stated in 1596, just 87 years after Columbus' first voyage to the Caribbean, "I was present at the beginning of the conquest of these regions and islands...so swiftly have they increased that the land seems to have taken vengeance and grown too narrow for them."

During the era of exploration, European countries sought to find a direct trade route to Asia to obtain luxury goods, especially gold and spices. In addition to finding this trade route, in the late 15th and early 16th centuries, the Spanish were driven by the need to spread Christianity to the native peoples of the Americas. As a result, the Spanish exploration of the Americas led to a dramatic increase in the global population. With the movement of people from Europe to the Americas, millions of people would mingle that had never met before.

The Columbian Exchange was a widespread exchange of animals, plants, culture, human populations (including slaves), communicable diseases, and ideas between the Eastern and Western hemispheres. It was one of the most significant events concerning ecology, agriculture, and culture in all of human history. The Columbian Exchange greatly affected the human and natural environment of the New and Old Worlds.

In 1492, Christopher Columbus sailed from Spain across the Atlantic Ocean to find a new trade route to Asia. Contrary to his expectations, he landed in what we know as the Bahamas and later explored the islands of present-day Cuba and Hispaniola (Dominican Republic). Though he was not successful in finding a route to Asia, his voyages to the Caribbean did have significant impacts on Europe and the Americas. The voyages of Columbus prompted the Spanish to explore and colonize the Americas and initiated the global exchange of goods, a process which is known as the Columbian Exchange.

5.1. Christopher Columbus

Columbus and his men were mistreated by the local islanders, and tensions increased due to their demands for food and resources. This behavior, and the actions of other European explorers who followed in Columbus' footsteps, instigated a pattern of aggression between the invaders and the native islanders, rapidly leading to complete destruction of the island's inhabitants and culture. Replicas of this pattern occurred continuously in the Americas where European explorers went on to 'discover'. This negative behavior was in deep contrast to the ideology of Spain and the monarchs, who had initially called for the peaceful and harmonious merging of Spanish and native cultures to create a more godly and civilized society. Due to the intense rivalry between European powers in the 15th and 16th centuries, high pressure was placed upon explorers to claim new lands for their empires. The ambiguity of the native peoples' humanity and rights created an atmosphere of free reign in the Americas, where explorers were allowed to get away with almost anything in the name of King and Church. This gave them an unbridled sense of authority, and allowed them to cause terrible harm and suffering to the native peoples, as demonstrated on numerous occasions by the likes of Columbus and his men. This occurrence would change the Americas forever and would set the stage for Spanish colonization in the New World.

5.2. Spanish Conquistadors

The first conquest was of the island of Hispaniola by the explorer Christopher Columbus. The island served as a base for military expeditions. Within a few years, the Spanish had conquered the native Taino people and taken complete control of the island. The Spanish then carried out conquests of Puerto Rico and Cuba. A whole generation of future conquistadors cut their teeth in the Caribbean. They would all dream of making names for themselves in the empires further west.

The Spanish conquistadors were soldiers of fortune in search of glory and riches. These men were the new men of the sixteenth century who were seeking adventure. They were inspired by the successful voyages that were bringing back treasures from the Americas. The conquest of a great empire that was rich in resources was considered the best way to both serve the empire and achieve personal wealth. The conquest of the Aztec and Incan empires is the stuff of legend.

5.3. English Explorers

In 1578, the privateering exploits of Sir Humphrey Gilbert and the expedition of Martin Frobisher in search of a northwest passage to the Orient marked the beginning of that famous, but elusive, sixteenth-century ambition to voyage across the North Atlantic in a northerly direction. Frobisher's three voyages, ending in 1578, 1577, and 1578, were Robert Dudley and the formation in 1579 of an association of London merchants, among which was Raleigh and the Queen's aid, gave it the form of an organized effort. This great project was merely one subsidiary feature of a grandiose world-wide scheme of imperialist expansion, and it signally failed. Frobisher found no way through the labyrinth of the Canadian Arctic islands.

In 1553, Sir Humphrey Gilbert put forward a plan for the discovery of rich and unknown lands to the west in the possession of the empire of the Spaniards. It was Gilbert's firm belief that England could best harass the power of Spain by attacking her colonial empire. He was, therefore, a forerunner of Drake, Raleigh, and others who set out to plunder Spanish America.

Cabot made another voyage in search of a westward passage to the East. In 1497 and 1498, he explored the coast of North America under the commission of Henry VII. He believed that the rich Oriental cities of Asia could be reached by sailing west from England. When it became clear that there was no direct passage to the East by this route, England lost interest in North America. John Cabot and his son disappeared on their second or third voyage and he was never heard from again.

CHAPTER 6

Exploration of Africa

The initial reception to the Portuguese was an encouraging one: they had met, on the whole, a group of sedentary city-states with which to trade. A ruling contrast was encountered with Malindi and its sworn enemy, Mombasa. The latter's Sultan had, through a conspiracy involving the massacre of twenty-four Portuguese, made an example of the kind of resistance that was to come through. This rebellion was met with the intended equivalent, sacking the town after regicide. Portugal's wane following Spain's annexation in 1580 meant there would be no follow-up to that short-lived empire on the East African coast, a legacy that is still apparent. The Portuguese then made an attempt to set up a fort at Sofala in 1505, intended to facilitate trade in gold with the inland Monomotapa Empire. This was to be a short-lived settlement whose cause was not helped by the Korean War-type situation the Portuguese found with extensive Chinese supplies being given to a native uprising and Zimbabwean counterattack.

The Portuguese were determined to have a route to Asia that circumvented the Arab middlemen. They were not originally fixated on the southern tip of Africa, but circumstances in the 1490s would change this. When the Cape of Good Hope was finally rounded in 1497 by Vasco da Gama, the route to Asia by sea was effectively discovered. Da

Gama had landed in modern-day Kenya and would further expose the East African coast to frequent Portuguese invasion.

6.1. Portuguese Explorers

Prince Henry was the fourth son of King João I, and master of the military Order of Christ. He never went on any exploration himself, and with the exception of the brief occupation of Ceuta in 1415, he was never interested in acquiring territory. His main aims were to spread Christianity and increase Portuguese influence. His understanding of geography made him realize that the wind system of the Eastern Atlantic, which allowed for easy return journeys, and the African coastal currents provided the means to explore south of the Saharan barrier.

The Portuguese exploration of Africa began in the mid-fifteenth century, with the desire to bypass the Muslim states and the lucrative spice trade. Most important was the capture of Ceuta in 1415 as it provided the impetus for the exploration of West Africa. Under Prince Henry the Navigator, Portugal had a long maritime lead over all other nations, and with it the ability to explore both the Atlantic arch and the African coast with relative freedom.

6.2. African Explorers

The Arabs were interested in spreading the word of Islam and often marrying African women as a means of converting local chiefs. Due to the fact that they were primarily interested in spreading religion, the Arabs were not very interested in mapping out the interior of Africa. However, there were a few exceptions, such as Sultan Moussa of Kilwa who, in 1321, hired Persian scholar Shaykh Abul-Fath to map his territories, and David Livingstone who, much later in the mid-19th century, would become world famous for his extensive exploration and zeal for spreading Christianity.

The African explorers were mostly of Arab descent and were made up of the interesting group known as the Swahili. It was a group of mixed race, their name derived from the Arabic word meaning "people of the coast". They were a mix of Arab and African, and their culture was very interesting, combining both Arab and Bantu essence. They were quite eager to explore and were driven by the massive trade network of East Africa. By working with Muslim traders, they soon adopted Islam and became quite literate, with several keeping diaries of their travels.

CHAPTER 7

Exploration of Asia

In 1421, a book by Gavin Menzies explores a theory that the Chinese had sailed to America before Columbus. Although the popular belief is that Chinese explorations were abruptly cancelled, evidence suggests that Admiral Zheng He had actually ordered the removal of all records of his expeditions, and Chinese shipbuilding had now shifted to larger land ships. Though the true reason is unknown, it can be seen that during this time, China was threatened by the Mongol Empire and Japanese pirates, and there was misinterpretation of Taoism by the collapse of the Confucian government. Fearing foreign invasion, Ming China tightened foreign contact, causing their voyages to end, and no current history before the eighteenth century has yet to offer solid information of China interacting with foreigners. Offered theories for the abrupt halt to foreign contact often label the Ming dynasty as isolationist, a failure in colonization, or inadequate military and economic strength to compete with other rivals.

From the fifteenth century, beginning with the Ming dynasty, China went through a period of naval exploration. Chinese junks went as far as East Africa and the Middle East. China had a great curiosity about parts of the world far beyond their borders.

7.1. *Portuguese Explorers*

The Portuguese circumnavigation of Africa and opening of a new sea route to Asia was a disaster for Muslims who had enjoyed a virtual monopoly of the Asian trade for centuries. This let the Portuguese force their way to Asia and create the global spice empire. The cost of war in Asia was great, as it supported a huge war machine for some time, but the benefits were extraordinary, leading to a shift in the European balance of power and the final crippling of the Muslim hold on Asia and the Indian Ocean.

By the end of the 16th century, Portugal's guarantee of economic gain around the Cape of Good Hope in Africa led them to build an empire incredibly quickly throughout Asia, Africa, and the Americas. With political and social reasons combined, trade was by far one of the most important aspects as to why and what the Portuguese explored. It was due to the pretense of creating a trading post empire, catching the Muslims and later the Turks between a pincer movement from the newborn European empires with blockage of the Red Sea and Persian Gulf. The Portuguese would eventually define a strategy to occupy key points to damage the enemy's chance to trade, all the way to the blockade at Suez.

Portugal was a dominant empire in the 16th century. It initiated major developments that caused Europe and the rest of the world to make a number of changes. At the time, Portugal was determined to find a direct sea route to Asia for trade. With valuable goods and stores of gold and silver, surely the rest of Europe would want to follow their advancements to ensure they had regular, not expensive, access to Asian goods.

7.2. *Chinese Explorers*

Zheng's fleets reached places from Korea to Sumatra, and from there he established Chinese maritime dominance. Tribute was gained from the vassal states and their acknowledgement of Chinese superiority. His largest achievement, however, was in the Indian Ocean where he estab-lished Chinese control. This nearly led to the colonization of Malacca.

Yet it was decided that there was no need to establish colonies, and so China left no long-term presence.

The seven voyages were remarkable for their time, being very long and over a large distance. The voyages were made between (1405-1407), (1407-1409), (1409-1411), (1413-1415), and the final voyage in (1431-1433). The fleet was massive, with around 300 ships and 28,000 sailors. The ship design was much more advanced than those of the Europeans, with the biggest ships being eight times longer than Christopher Columbus' Santa Maria.

Zheng He was a Muslim eunuch who became a superior court official of the Ming Emperor. The Emperor was a great supporter of naval power and sent Zheng on these missions to seek new tributaries who would acknowledge the emperor's superiority. Spreading Chinese influence and receiving tribute are often mentioned as the main reasons for his ventures. However, more recently it has been suggested that the motive was to form a defensive ring around China. This was because the Mongol hordes had previously been repelled by Japan and the Japanese had then sought to attack China.

Zheng He (1371-1433) was an extraordinary admiral and explorer who made key discoveries for China. Although his name in Chinese means "peaceful and virtuous one", Zheng was an effective military leader who won great battles for the Ming Emperor. However, his name has lived on because of the seven occasions in the early 15th century when he led a vast fleet of ships through the Indian Ocean and beyond.

7.3. Dutch Explorers

The Dutch East India Company. It was in the realm of commerce that the Dutch made their most notable contribution to the work of the world. In the days of the ascendancy of the Sea Power "Greater Britain," it is perhaps not easy for us to realize that there was a time when England's great overseas empire did not exist. Yet, when the Dutch republic was at the zenith of its power, it was for a brief moment mistress of the oversea trade of the world and bade fair to establish a world-empire of a new type. This it proposed to do by the same method by which Portugal and Spain had essayed to make their vast and scattered dominions more than a mere memory. The end of the War of Independence found the Dutch united and inspired by a lofty sense of what they had already achieved and what the future might have in store. They were drawn by the tide of a great hope, great as any that had actuated the princes of the Renaissance. Like Spain and Portugal in their great decades, the victorious republic proposed to win its way to glory by an expansion of the New Birth of Freedom and a new sort of world-dominion which it should exemplify. And, as the most certain means to this end, and as a worthy sequel to its heroic past, the little commonwealth elected to build itself an empire; and it was of this, that it should not on a globe-embracing dominion, there brooded the War of Thirty Years, which was in the words of Frederick the Great, "a war of all the world."

History did not allow the Dutch as much time as it did the Portuguese to carry through their plans for a far-flung empire. The greater part of their career as the dominant sea power was passed while their struggle for independence was yet unfinished. In glory and in misery, in victory and in defeat, the tiny republic was forced to concentrate upon the winning of its life in the narrow space between land and sea which remained to it. But the fact that the Dutch had neither time nor opportunity to follow up the achievements of their great seamen by constructing a world-empire of their own should not be allowed to obscure the importance of the part which they played in the general history of exploration during the seventeenth century.

CHAPTER 8

Scientific Discoveries and Advancements

Botany and zoology also made considerable progress during the Age of Exploration. With the increased overseas contact, many new plant and animal specimens were brought back to Europe for study. The priests and monks who often accompanied the explorers frequently took an interest in the new flora and fauna, and many natural history collections were made as a result of their efforts. This led to an increased desire to systematize the study of natural history, and a need for the foundation of a science which would later become known as biology. The medicinal value of the new plants was of special interest to the physicians and an extensive study was made of their practical uses. This knowledge also contributed to the art of pharmacology and the development of new medicines. During the 16th century, the Holy Roman Emperor, Rudolf II, established a botanical garden in Prague for the cultivation of rare plants, and in the 17th century similar gardens were founded in Italy and France. This era also saw the introduction of the scientific study of animals, and in 1592 the Swiss naturalist, Konrad Gesner, published Historia Animalium, which attempted to encompass all of human knowledge of animals in a single work, and is considered the beginning of modern zoology.

This vast knowledge of the planets and stars has brought us a long, long way since ancient times. And the developments made during the Age of Exploration have played a significant role in shaping the world as we know it today. But this renaissance of astronomical knowledge was not limited to the European nations. During the 17th century, the Mughal Empire in India produced a catalogue of stars in which the scientist determined the positions of equinoxes, and some 200 years later another Indian astronomer accurately calculated the precession of the equinoxes. In China, the Emperor allowed the Jesuits to continue their work in mapping the heavens in the hope that an understanding of western astronomy would help the Chinese revise their traditional calendar. As a result, the Chinese astronomers produced maps of the stars in both the traditional Chinese format and in the European style. This information was later compiled into the Treatise of the Astronomy of the Chinese, and proved valuable for western astronomers who were trying to determine the relationship between the Chinese and Julian calendars. The culmination of these efforts was the building of an observatory in Beijing, in 1644, which contained a unique combination of Chinese and European astronomical instruments.

8.1. Astronomy and Navigation

The magnetic compass, probably introduced to Europe through contact with the Arabs, Indians, or Chinese, was adapted for navigation at sea early in the 13th century. The compass provided a quick and reliable method of direction and was a perfect match for the course and distance method of dead reckoning. However, its interaction with the iron in ships' nails caused large errors and deviation. The compass was a nearly perfect method in determining direction, but the variation had to be understood. This was first done by the English in the mid-16th century and is still a fundamental part of navigation.

Early astronomers such as Galileo, Copernicus, and Kepler, though not explorers themselves, provided a crucial step for navigators to come. The development of astronomical observatories and more precise instruments rapidly increased the understanding of celestial phenomena.

This formed the basis of what is now known as celestial navigation: the use of angular measurements between celestial bodies to determine position and direction.

An understanding of the Earth was gained through increased knowledge of the surrounding universe. Astronomy and the development of navigational instruments were two important offshoots of the Age of Discovery. As sailors and explorers sought to find new trade routes and new lands, they were forced to travel longer distances and for longer spans of time. This necessitated a more accurate understanding of the skies for celestial navigation, and more reliable methods of determining time and direction.

8.2. Botany and Zoology

Young Oviedo and Cieza de León, both of them soldiers, were among the first to collect botanical specimens. The first named began this work at San Domingo in 1535, and the other, with his enthusiastic treasurer, Gonzalo Pizarro, at Cartagena and other places on the Isthmus. In connection with his conquests in South America, Pizarro's name is associated with a curious zoological misunderstanding. Having heard from the Indians of the existence of a bird whose pork-like flesh was greatly esteemed, Pizarro inquired of various Portuguese in the expedition what this could be. He learned from them again and again the word "pato," which means duck, though they intended to speak of the bird as "pato real," king duck. He concluded that hog and bird were identical and sent to Spain the celebrated message, "Send me breeding stock of those pigs which eat and rest in trees." Its only result was to draw from the monkey, Xerez, which lived to chronicle the deeds of its master, a gibe which became a well-known Spanish proverb, "Thus it is with fine words today and action tomorrow." His kinsman, Hernando Pizarro, after the conquest of Peru, accompanied Charles V on the ill-fated Algerine expedition of 1541, on which, having seen some large African apes, he sent to the monarch, who prided himself on his possession of strange creatures, a graphic picture of the apes with the request that the emperor would send him here its equal in a secretary.

His request was duly fulfilled, the secretary chosen being Dr. Ruy Diaz de Guzman, a distinguished member of the Royal Council of the Indies. Neither Hernando Pizarro nor his friends appreciated the sally, which owed its preservation to the discomfitures of the expedition, and the Guzman family resented it for some three generations. Yet the pastime of the gay donor reveals his sagacity, for Ruy Diaz was indeed an uncommon secretary, who needed but the prehensile tail to be imitable the apes of Algiers.

8.3. Cartography and Mapmaking

Some of the most crucial scientific advancements, mapmaking and cartography also underwent significant transformation. During the Age of Exploration, maps were changed from being simply statements of where coastlines were to being statements of political, theological, philosophical, and ideological claims to space. Europe used the representation of space and placement of boundaries on maps to claim superiority over other cultures, and during this era, the Europeans used maps to claim new territories in the undeveloped continents of the world. Theoretical claims have historically also been made on cosmological grounds, and through cartography, it was easy to represent the Earth as the center of the universe. In this way, the discoveries in cosmology also had a profound effect on the representation of the world in maps. With the Copernican shift in understanding the universe, the work of astronomers like Galileo and Kepler on the nature of the solar system and the shape of the Earth led to a radical change in the way Europeans thought about their world and subsequently how they represented it in maps. The practical needs of navigators, who in the early 15th century knew little more than the mariners of Ancient Greece, were important in the development of scientific mapmaking and the understanding of the shape, location, and size of the earth. Using the recent translations of the Geographia of Claudius Ptolemy from Greek into Latin, mapmakers were able to employ their new understanding of the earth as a starting point in the systematic representation of the geography of the known world. Printing technology made rapid advances in the 15th century so that maps and globes, plentiful by the 16th century, could be updated with new discoveries. The application of the method of longitude and latitude to the charting of the earth's surface, which had a profound effect on increasing the accuracy of marine charts, was an innovation of the Age of Discovery.

CHAPTER 9

The Consequences of Exploration

The consequences of the Age of Exploration were so impactful that they changed the entire world, transforming society systems into internationalism and leading to the development of technology and science. The first and biggest impact is internationalism, which means the strong relationship between countries involving cooperation to reach certain purposes for salvation that have been defined together. This phenomenon didn't occur on one or two continents, but now it occurs all over the world. It started with colonialism, where countries from Europe, which had advanced technology at that time, wanted to expand their influence and gain as much wealth as possible by exploiting regions outside their own countries. They used military, economic, political, and cultural means to build lasting relationships. Colonialism caused a lot of wars between countries, mergers between different societies and traditions, and resistance from civil society. This led to the formation of a new global system that still sustains until now.

Today, the global integration between societies is overwhelmingly huge because it has been two long eras of immersion between those societies. The first era was the exploration led by Christopher Columbus in 1492, which finally ended in the 18th century. This exploration occurred in every part of the world, including America, Europe, Africa, and Asia, and is known as the "Age of Discovery" or "Age of Exploration". There are plenty of impacts that still sustain until now and change the entire world, especially in terms of cultural and societal systems.

9.1. Columbian Exchange

The "Columbian Exchange" has been called the single most important event in the history of the world, largely because it brought two separate worlds (Old World and New World) together and mixed both biologically and culturally. This exchange greatly shaped the modern world. The Columbian Exchange of crops affected both the Old World and the New. Amerindian crops that have changed the world include tomatoes, potatoes, and maize. The Old World gained from the New World crops such as tobacco, cocoa, and most importantly maize which became a staple crop. Maize also vastly increased agricultural yields in the Old World. Perhaps most importantly, the Old World received two staple crops, cassava and sweet potato, from the New World. These crops are important in that they are a source of cheap carbohydrates for the common people. A side effect of the Columbian Exchange of crops was the great population explosion of the Old World. The exchange of animals also greatly affected the New World and the Old. The introduction of Old World animals greatly changed life for Amerindians. In South America, horses utterly changed the lifestyle and hunting capabilities of the Plains Indians. In what is now the United States and Canada, the introduction of horses and of Old World crops and livestock had a profound impact on the native cultures in these regions. The Amerindians were introduced to many new technologies and European lifestyle, however they very often adopted these things while retaining much of their old cultural traditions. One of the New World animals had a far more negative impact on the Amerindians. The introduction of rats to the New World had disastrous effects for the natives, because rats were carriers of diseases to which the Amerindians had no immunity, and therefore rats helped rapidly kill off a large portion of the Amerindian population. The effects on the Old World from the exchange of New World animals and crops were no less profound. The introduction of maize to Europe increased agricultural yields; before potatoes became widespread, maize was the most productive yield crop known. Maize and the huge amounts of silver from the New World that poured into Spain caused a population explosion and economic revival in Spain. The economic effects of maize were felt as far away as the Indian sub-continent, Africa and Indonesia, where it served as an easily grown crop which could feed both humans and livestock.

9.2. Colonization and Imperialism

An additional method the Europeans used to colonize during the time of the new imperialism was the establishment of colonies in which unwanted people from the motherland would migrate to. This was used mainly in Latin America, where the Spanish and Portuguese would help alleviate social ills in their homelands by shipping these people off to the colonies to be laborers.

The scramble for Africa best illustrates the new imperialism. In its recognition between the powers lived a situation of tension and latent violence in which only a provocation or a wind of accident was needed to kindle an explosion. The Europeans, with the discovery of vast untapped natural resources and a small amount of resistance, "carved up the African continent with little regard for her many different inhabitants" and declared the sparsely populated or uninhabited lands as terra nullis. The Europeans would force the native inhabitants to leave by a variety of methods and claim the land as their own. Direct control was then established within these areas and large numbers of European peoples would settle and colonize the area. This method was also prevalent in the Americas, Australia, and New Zealand.

The new imperialism was the modern form of colonization. Although the basic concept of the two are the same, the new imperialism took on a much larger scale and was much more violent.

During the time of the old imperialism, the main goal of the European nations was to create a strong economic presence in Asia. In order to achieve this goal, the Europeans set up trading posts where the primary purpose was to act as a base for the much larger and more powerful European armies. These armies would then be used to enact national control over that area. At this point, direct control was established within the area not by migrating people from the stronger nation to the weaker one, but by economically exploiting the weaker nation's resources and people. This method was especially prevalent in India. The reason that the Europeans did not fully colonize these areas during the time of the old imperialism was because the immense distance from their homeland to these countries made permanent settlement with a significant number of people impractical.

Colonization is the direct extension of national sovereignty and control by a strong country over a weaker one. The goals are to exploit the natural resources and the native inhabitants of the weaker territories. The methods and motives of colonization between the old and new imperialism greatly differ.

9.3. Cultural Exchange and Globalization

This section focuses on the role of cultural exchange and interaction starting with the Columbian voyages, and the lasting effects that the emergence of a truly global culture had on the various civilizations involved. Early cultural exchanges were, for the most part, unintentional conquests by the colonizers that were met with strong resistance by the indigenous people as their lands and traditions. The staggering death toll of the native population caused by the introduction of new diseases would haunt the Americas for generations and significantly weaken their ability to resist the European incursion during later years. The decimation of the local populace necessitated the importation of slaves from Africa and indentured servants from Europe to fill the void of labor needed to make the New World exploitable for the mother countries. This introduced a new wave of cultural interaction between the races and social classes, often leading to fusion of cultures between the conquerors and the conquered as well as the creation of new social and racial classifications. The introduction of the African people to the Americas represents one of the largest forced migrations in history; it is estimated that a third of the complete the voyage. This massive transfer of people and cultures had a profound impact on both continents. The Africans, often already possessing immunity to many of the diseases of the Americas, quickly became the dominant exploited class as the native population continued to wither. Their rich and diverse cultures would significantly influence the cultures of both Americas and Europe in unexpected ways. This impact is most obvious in the Caribbean and Latin America where large mixed race populations are the result of centuries of interbreeding between the races. The rich cultures of these regions are often syncretic fusions of European, indigenous, and African elements. In places like Brazil and Haiti, the slave population would actually manage to create societies independent of the European influence. This age of globalization had a profound impact on the modern world; for better or worse, much of what has occurred in the world in the past five centuries can be attributed to it.

CHAPTER 10

Legacy of the Age of Discovery

The voyages of discovery had several significant effects on Europe. It greatly increased the Europeans' knowledge and power. However, the people living in the lands Europeans "discovered" were to a large extent adversely affected. The process of discovery had a marked effect on the world both then and now. The voyages of discovery had more negative effects for the indigenous peoples of the lands "discovered". With the vision of spreading Christianity, the Europeans could be extremely fanatical in attempts to convert indigenous peoples. This could lead to all-out war on the indigenous population, and in many cases such as the Spanish conquest of the Americas, the Europeans were victorious, slaughter and enslavement followed, and a world which was only years before vast and open to the people living there now became smaller and foreign. Also, with the new land discoveries, the European powers looked to each other to stake territorial claims, leading again to war in which the native population was often forced to take sides. The transmission of diseases which greatly affected the indigenous populations of the lands "discovered" was not intentional, however, it proved to be the most devastating effect of discovery. The fewer cases of smallpox prior to the first successful oceanic voyage spread a wave of smallpox throughout the now easily traveled lands. This was seen in 1518 in what is now Mexico, where fever and sores afflicted the people and created so much illness that many died and could no longer tend their crops. At the arrival of the Spanish conquistadors, they found the land to be more sparsely populated and many Aztecs and their emperor Montezuma had attributed the illness to be a sign of an impending disaster or even the end of the world. This facilitated the Spanish conquest of the Aztec empire and with various cases of similar disasters throughout the lands discovered, the ease of conquest for the Europeans was due to weakened indigenous populations. It is argued that what followed conquest, be it enslavement or outright slaughter, was generally not the intention of the European powers, but the wants of explorers and later settlers were often put ahead of the interests of the native population. This led to an era of European dominance and marked the start of the globalization of the world, an effect which has continued to this day.

10.1. Impact on World History

The most evident aspect of the impact of the age of great explorations on world history is the establishment of European hegemony in the world. European expansion would lead to the construction of a global system, bringing the world's societies into interaction with one another—no single event would have a greater long-term effect on the inhabitants of the Americas, Africa, Asia and Oceania. European global dominance was achieved between Columbus' time and the present through a process that included, among others, the establishment of maritime empires and the initiation of an export-import economy. European economic and military power was translated into political control and social dominance over the rest of the world. Europe and the world would never be the same.

The age of the great explorations had far-reaching effects on world history. The western European nations, on the threshold of the modern era, sought alternate routes to the rich trade of Asia. They were also driven by a fervent desire to expand the boundaries of Christendom. The accidental discoveries of new lands and peoples by explorers searching for routes to Asia sparked a series of developments that would have global implications. The early explorations along the African coast and into the Atlantic were discussed in terms of their impact on Iberian society and the initiative for further expansion. These repercussions also weighed heavily in England, France and the Netherlands, as well as in other areas such as the Swedes' search for a northeast passage and the Russians' exploration of Siberia.

10.2. Exploration in the Modern Era

In its broadest form, this last age of discovery was a part of that western expansion, which began with the voyages of Columbus. Explorers were still engaged in the task of finding out what the world is like, and they still sought geographic knowledge for many of the same geographical and political reasons. The English were looking for the Northwest passage to the north. The Spaniards were still searching for the unattained limits of El Dorado and the southeastern frontier of their empire in Peru. The Portuguese explorations into the vast unknown regions between Brazil and Asia were a part of a plan to round out their claims to the Eastern Hemisphere. Many of these quests had no small effect upon the modern world. The second voyage of Captain Cook, for example, was in part an attempt to find a cure for scurvy. The commercial value of such a cure was inestimable, and it was largely in hopes of gaining a mastery of the South Seas as a healthful environment for its crews that Britain gave up its claims in Australia. In the hundreds of years that the problem of a southern land route to the Pacific, it had been the Uruguay question that determined the policy of Spain in South America.

The period of discovery did not end with the closing of the fifteenth century. New lands were still being found, and the search for land trade routes to Asia and the Indies remained a goal. For the most part, however, the geography of the world was known after Columbus' time, and the problem that remained was largely one of filling in the outlines of the map. The story of the discovery that the known world was only a part of the whole and the story of the exploration of the lands beyond the sea routes to the East belongs to the modern era. This modern era of discovery began around the middle of the eighteenth century and it too was an age of scientific exploration.